I Love Me Some Me

I0110954

Written by Tracey A. Mash

Illustrated by Alex Alston

Copyright © 2024 Tracey A. Mash. All rights reserved.

All rights reserved. Printed in the United States of America. No part of this book may be used or reproduced in any manner whatsoever without written permission except in the case of brief quotations embodied in critical articles and reviews.

Scripture taken from the HOLY BIBLE, NEW INTERNATIONAL VERSION. Copyright 1973, 1978, 1984 by International Bible Society. Used by permission of Zondervan Publishing House. All rights reserved.

The "NIV" and "New International Version" trademarks are registered in the United States Patent and Trademark Office by International Bible Society. Use of either trademark requires the permission of International Bible Society.

ISBN: 979-8-89109-911-1 (paperback)
ISBN: 979-8-89109-910-4 (hardcover)
ISBN: 979-8-89109-912-8 (ebook)

This book is dedicated to my amazing grandchildren, Dyamond, JaQuay, Neriah, Kamrion, Carmelo, and Kadence. I LOVE ME SOME YOU!

Hi, my name is Kadence. I am 9 years old, and I LOVE ME SOME ME!

I love my skin! It looks like the
color of caramel candy.

2

I love the color of my family and friends' skin and
others whose skin color is different from mine.
Do you love your skin?
What does your skin look like?

I love my hair! I can wear it naturally
curly, braided, twisted, straightened
out, and in so many other ways.

I love my family and friends' hair and others
whose hair is different from mine.
Do you love your hair? What are some
ways you can wear your hair?

I love the shape and color of my eyes!
My eyes are brown and sort of shaped like an
almond. My Grammy taught me how to wink.

I love the shape and color of my family
and friends' eyes and others whose shapes
and colors are different from mine.
Do you love the shape and color of
your eyes? Can you wink?

I love the shape of my ears! My Poppi
(this is what I call my grandfather) taught
me how to make them wiggle.

I love the shape
of my family and
friends' ears and
others whose ears are
shaped differently from mine.
Do you love the shape of your ears?
Can you make your ears wiggle?

wiggle

I love the shape of my nose!
I can make it move.

I love the shape of my family and friends' noses
and others whose noses are different from mine.
Do you love the shape of your nose?
Can you make your nose move?

I love the shape of my lips!
My daddy taught me how to whistle.

I love the shape of my family and friends' lips
and others whose lips are different from mine.
Do you love the shape of your lips?
Can you whistle? Blow a bubble?

I love my hands! I use them to pick up things like my dog Nicklaus.

I love my family and friends' hands and others whose hands are different from mine. Do you love your hands? What are some fun things you can do with your hands?

I love my fingers!
I can tickle my brothers with them.

I love my family and friends' fingers and others whose fingers are different from mine. Do you love your fingers? What can you do with your fingers?

I love my legs!
I can dance, run, and jump with them.

I love my family and friends' legs and others
whose legs are different from mine.
Do you love your legs? What can
you do with your legs?

I love my toes! Mommy and I like to get them polished. Pink is my favorite color.

I love my family and friends' toes and others whose toes are different from mine. Do you love your toes? What can you do with your toes?

I love people who look like me ...

and those who don't!

23

I love people who speak the same language as I do ...

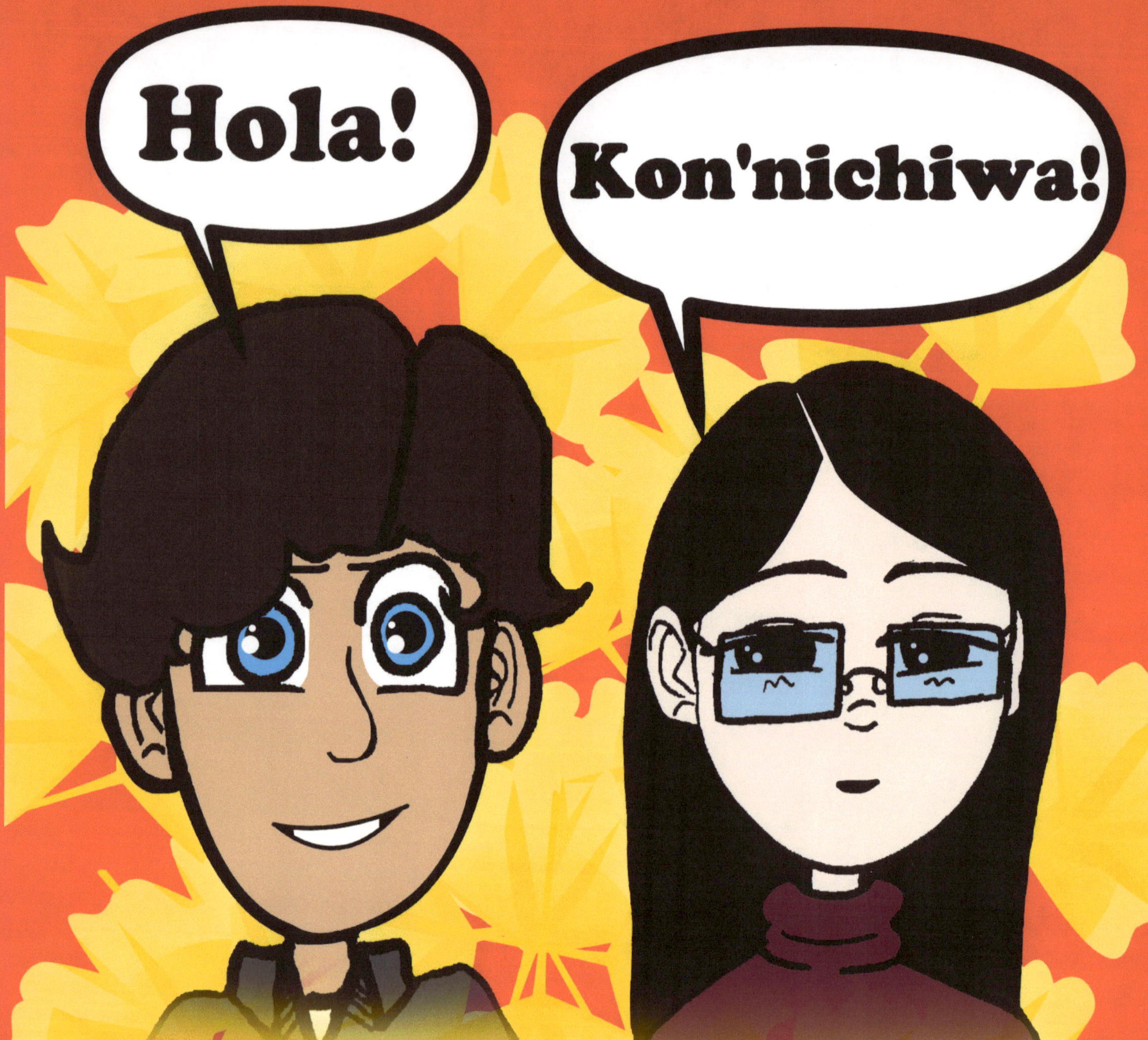

and those who don't!

But most of all, I LOVE that
I LOVE MYSELF because it teaches
me how to LOVE others!

Love is patient.
Love is kind.
Love is not jealous of what other people have.
Love does not brag about what you have.
Love is not proud.
Love is not rude to others.
Love looks out for others.
Love does not get mad easily.
Love does not hold grudges.
Love does not like mistreatment
but is happy with the truth.
Love always protects.
Love always trusts.
Love always hopes.
Love always keeps going.
Love never lets you down.

1 Corinthians 13:4–8a NIV

I love people who look like me...

and those who don't.

I love people who speak the same language as I do...

and those who don't.

But most of all, I LOVE that I LOVE MYSELF because it teaches me how to LOVE others!

(Draw a picture of yourself)

AUTHOR BIO

Tracey A. Mash is the author of *Morning Glories* and has now written her first children's book titled *I Love Me Some Me*. *I Love Me Some Me* is about loving oneself and loving the differences in all of us.

Tracey's hometown is St. Louis, Missouri; she currently lives in La Vernia, Texas, with her husband, Donald. They are the grandparents to six amazing grandchildren.

ABOUT THE ILLUSTRATOR

Alex Alston was born in Japan and raised in San Antonio. He has been drawing since he was 6 years old. Alex has published work as an illustrator on Amazon such as Tea Time with Jesus, Inspired to Sing, and his own comics, Alston Adventures. He is the owner of Alex Alston's Awesome Art and Bandit Comix, an art and comic business which he runs through Facebook. For more information about Alex Alston's work visit the following: www.alstonadventurez.biz, Facebook@Alex Alston's Awesome Art, and Tik-tok@mr.alextheartist

A BIG "THANK YOU"

For Reading My Book!

I really appreciate all of your feedback and
I love hearing what you have to say.

If this book has made you and/or your child smile
I would love your input.

Please take two minutes now to leave a
helpful review on Amazon letting me know
what you thought about the book.

Thank you so much!

TRACEY A. MASH

www.ingramcontent.com/pod-product-compliance
Lightning Source LLC
LaVergne TN
LVHW072105070426
835508LV00003B/268